CW00326741

Insider
Information

Published by MQ Publications Limited
12 The Ivories, 6–8 Northampton Street, London N1 2HY
Tel: 020 7359 2244 / Fax: 020 7359 1616
email: mail@mqpublications.com

ISBN: 1-84072-517-6

1 3 5 7 9 0 8 6 4 2

Printed and bound in China

Insider Information

How the office really works

BY LISA SWERLING & RALPH LAZAR

MQP

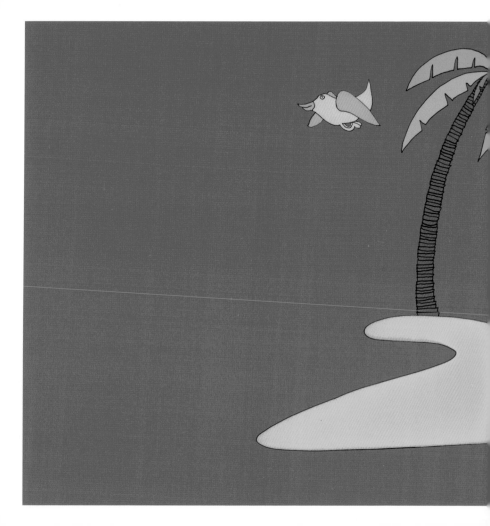

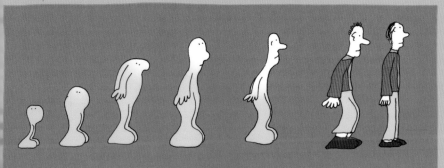

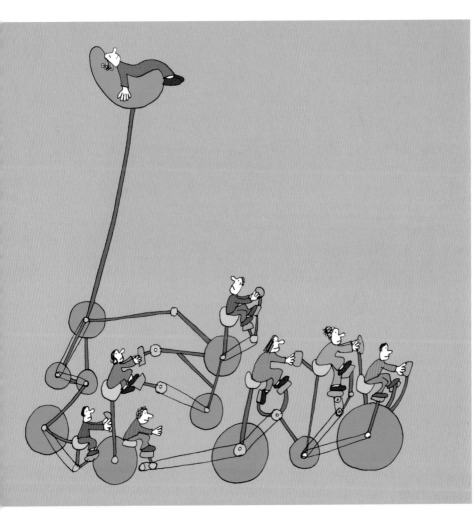

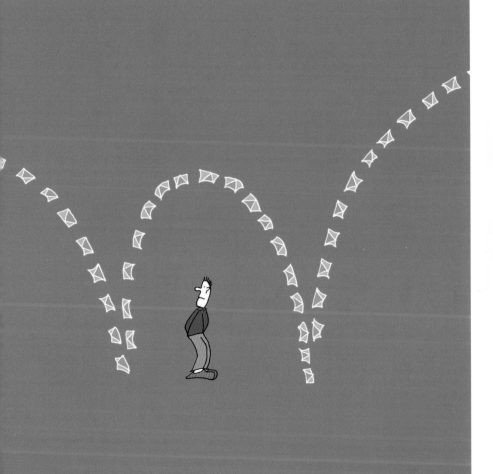

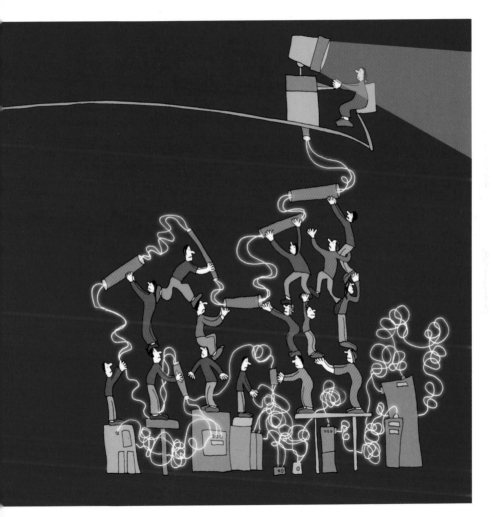

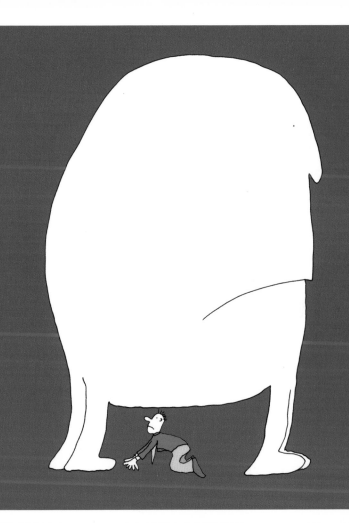

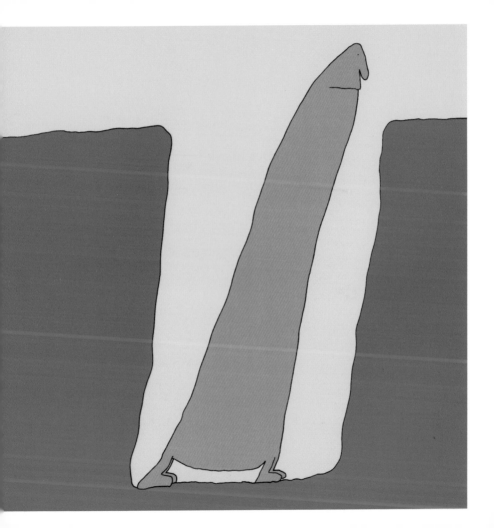

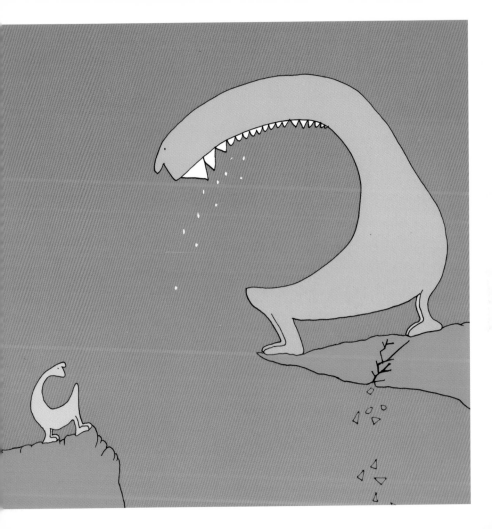

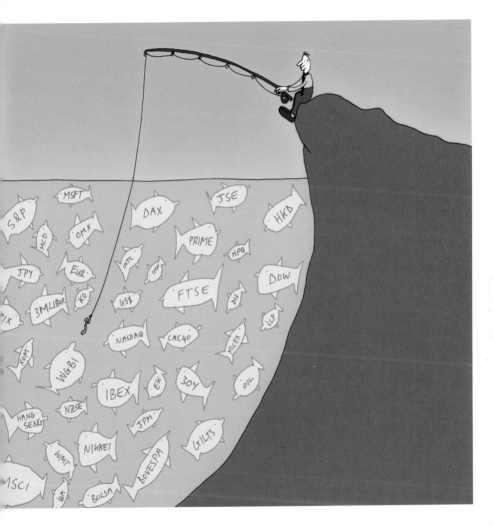

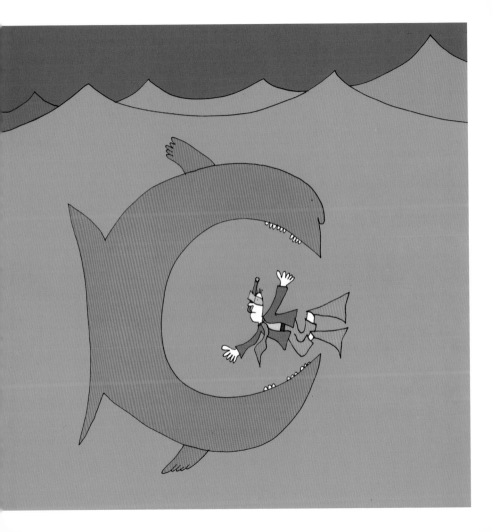

ABOUT THE AUTHORS

Ralph Lazar and Lisa Swerling are currently
based in the UK. Other series created by them
include Harold's Planet and Hotdog-Dog.